GW00394315

CAN YOU HEAR

A Handbook on Voice for All who Teach

Text by Caroline Cornish

Drawings by John H. Bartlett

With a Foreword by Professor Ted Wragg

First published in Great Britain by **BiVocal Press** 1995
148 Heavitree Road, Exeter EX1 2LZ

Copyright Text © Caroline Cornish 1995
Copyright Illustrations © John H. Bartlett 1995
Copyright Foreword © Professor E. C. Wragg 1995

British Library Cataloguing in Publication Data. A catalogue
record for this book is available from the British Library.

ISBN 0 9526458 0 7

All rights reserved. No part of this publication may be reproduced,
stored in a retrieval system, or transmitted, in any form or by any
means, electronic, mechanical, photocopying, recording or otherwise
without the prior permission in writing of the publishers.

Acknowledgement and thanks

This book has been a long time in the making, but
during its gestation I have been constantly supported
(and nagged) by my family and friends. I thank them
for not relinquishing the hope that it would one day see
the light of day.

I owe a special debt of gratitude to Sally O'Shea,
whose unfailing interest and encouragement (to say nothing
of keyboard skills) kept me at it when the going was tough.

I acknowledge the good cheer of William Pattinson,
Headteacher, invaluable advice from Drummond Johnston,
and the generosity of Chris Scott for his
perpetual loan of the computer, and his endless patience.

Special thanks to Nigel Weaver for his help and
technical expertise.

Lastly and mostly for that long line of students who,
over the years have provided me with the questions to be
answered and the needs to be met.

Here it is then for all of you.

Remembering Jane
and for Fred

With love and gratitude

FOREWORD

I have only lost my voice once when teaching. It was a few weeks after I began my career. Having no voice for a couple of days taught me the meaning of the term 'non-verbal communication'. I began by writing on the board "I have lost my voice". Class erupts with mirth. So I wrote underneath "and the next person to laugh is in detention for a week". Silence. After that it was all gestures and mimes.

Teaching is much easier *with* a voice than without one. The teacher's voice is like the professional violinist's violin. Like a Stradivarius it should be looked after and used carefully.

Caroline Cornish has a lifetime of experience helping new, and experienced, teachers get the best out of their Stradivarius. The reader is advised to pay heed to the ideas in this book for one very good reason. They work.

Professor E C Wragg
Exeter University

WHY THIS BOOK
An introduction

THE CHALLENGE
Why teachers talk / When they need to shout / How a book
may help / What is required

THE KIT
How the voice works / How we speak / Voice as instrument

THE REAL WORK
The body/voice connection / The exercises / Additional advice

SPACE TRAVEL
The scope of the job / What happens when you try too hard /
Better ways of coping with space / Projecting the voice /
Projecting the thought

TO WHOM IT MAY CONCERN
Different levels-different problems / The Lecturer / The
Secondary teacher / The Primary teacher

INDOORS AND OUT
The Hall / The Classroom / The Science lab / The Gym The Swimming pool / The Field

COLOURING IT IN
Dynamics / Emphasis / Tone of voice / The Unspoken word / The Considered word / Exercising the words / Next step / Pitch and Rhythm

READING ALOUD
Common faults / Proper aims / Sensible advice

STORY TELLING
From time immemorial / Usefulness of stories / More sensible advice

LOOKING AFTER IT
The Dry throat / The Circumstances / The Cure / Starting up / Winding down

THE LAST WORD
How it began / Why it changed / Sub-texts / Place of technique/ Past affects present / Final advice

WHY THIS BOOK

If you have a headache ... you take an aspirin.

       If your feet hurt ... you go to the chiropodist.

            If your car battery is flat ... you get a new one.

But if your voice aches, hurts or sounds flat and ineffective ... what do you do?

Can you take a pill, go to an expert or get a new one?

It's true that expert help is available, and if you have a serious or chronic problem you should seek proper treatment. But what if it's more an ongoing, niggling feeling that your voice tires too easily and doesn't seem to cut much ice?

Why then, you probably just keep going, vaguely dissatisfied, shrug and assume it's just the way things are, just the voice you have (no fault of your own). Maybe you feel envious of those who seem to speak effortlessly for hours and never get a sore throat. Voice-training, you tell yourself, is for actors, for public speakers, and you've heard that there are places where you can acquire that kind of expertise, learn the tricks of the trade ...

Now stop THERE!..... Wait a minute and think again ...

What trade are YOU in? If it's teaching, your voice is the prime tool of your trade. You are using your voice more than anyone, in any other job, anywhere ... and sometimes to its limits.

YOU are the person I am addressing ... YOU are the one for whom I am writing this book. Who is in need of a powerful and flexible instrument, well-tuned and able to serve you through many long years? ...

... YOU ARE.

Whether you are a student in training for the profession, a primary school teacher with the reception class, a middle school specialist, a secondary school teacher, a junior lecturer or a professor of long and learned standing, all of you, sooner or later want to know the answer to the question: CAN YOU HEAR ME AT THE BACK? ...

... and all of you are hoping for an affirmative reply.

THE CHALLENGE

Let's start by considering the teacher and the job itself. All of us (and I'm a teacher too) have similar vocal demands made on us, no matter in what situation, or at what level we teach. Content and method will vary; so will the degree of intensity, our expectations and the responses we get. But some factors remain constant.

The teacher is the person 'in charge': the one with the information and intelligence to impart, the wit and wisdom to share. Many different ways may be employed to achieve our ends; audio, visual, experiential, but there will always be talk, talk, and more talk.

You want to be able to do that talking easily, expressively, engagingly and authoritatively, without strain or discomfort. First and foremost, you want to be HEARD.

The title of this book was arrived at quite simply. The students who come to my door ask me the following questions with remarkable regularity.

'Can you teach me to shout?' ... Yes, that's what they actually ask me.
'Why is my throat so sore?' ... Why indeed?
'How can I be heard at the back?' ... A sensible question.
My first task is usually to explain that the solution to the last question is not an affirmation of the first!

I need to add here that shouting is occasionally a perfectly valid practice for the teacher; for example, 'Keep that flame away from that flask of hydrogen NOW!' or, 'Come down from there this INSTANT!'

Anything which threatens life and limb may have to be dealt with by the urgent shout. But it is not a method of utterance for ordinary classroom practice; bad for you, bad for them. The rare shout from a normally quietly- spoken teacher can be shockingly effective, but in repetition it loses impact, and diminishes you as a person, as well as wreaking havoc on your vocal tract.

There are better ways of being heard at the back ... and they can be learnt.

In an ideal world all teachers should have access to advice and guidance on how to make the best of their voices, both before they qualify and afterwards. There is no substitute for individual voice tuition, but group work with a properly trained voice teacher and a speech and language therapist is also excellent, and can be good fun into the bargain. Working with a group helps you listen more shrewdly, and the sharing of common problems is also therapeutic. Such workshops are on the increase and deserve to be supported.

But it's *not* an ideal world, so use this book as a reference source. It will explain how your voice works, point the way to better practice, and list some helpful exercises. It will make you think about the value and importance of giving due consideration to your voice, and provide you with a direction to follow. You always know when something you read applies to you. Identify these pitfalls and take advice about avoiding them. Try the exercises and see if they help. I offer different strategies for you to try which have been developed from my own teaching. A book provides a key to new ideas; it can be emboldening, and in exploring old ground you may discover new territory.

One of the problems for people like me is to persuade you that change is possible. I am not talking about transformation, although sometimes that happens. Every voice is unique. Nobody else has a voice exactly like yours; similar maybe, and within your family perhaps very similar, but yours is still absolutely special.

Voice-training is not about beautifying the sound, or acquiring a particular 'teaching' voice. It is about helping you realise its potential, about freeing it, about enabling your voice to meet the demands of the classroom. It's finding the strength and flexibility that you will need for the many roles a teacher has to play.

Teachers have always known the job was tough. Today it's probably tougher than ever. We have to find the best ways and means of dealing with it ...

That is the challenge.

THE KIT

Though we are born with a natural impulse to make sound, and eventually to join in with the speaking world by making very specific sounds, the way in which we do it is nothing short of miraculous. And like a good many miracles we tend to take it all for granted unless it doesn't do what we expect and 'lets us down'.

Our ability to speak is an evolutionary triumph. It is not a basic system like reproduction or circulation but one made up of bits and pieces from other systems, a job lot, a D.I.Y. creation, a masterpiece of adaptation.

Take breathing, for instance, which is our source of energy for vocalising. The breathing process is essential to life. We breathe to take oxygen in and get rid of unwanted carbon dioxide. That unwanted, outgoing airstream is what we use to activate the vocal cords. In fact, every time we speak, we are re-cycling a waste product; positively man's first effort in that direction.

How about the cords? (And they *are* spelt like that, contrary to popular opinion; journalists invariably endow them with a musical quality by calling them c<u>h</u>ords). The muscle tissue of which they are composed makes a breath-controlling valve in the larynx and it's my belief that we can think of that as its basic function. What happens when your car won't start on a chilly morning? You have to summon all your energy (or that of your neighbours) and push it down the nearest slope. You take a deep breath. By closing the valve you hold the air in your body which alters your blood pressure and increases your muscle power. Listen to yourself grunting each time you release the throat. Hear your voice being activated involuntarily. When you stub your toe or are struck from behind all your instincts for survival come into play. Reacting to pain and preparing to retaliate you close that valve, and on its release, we hear a yell, a howl or some other instinctive response. This could be a high or a low note; the elastic nature of the cords determines the frequency. The act of giving birth is often more dramatically noisy, and for precisely the same reason. Watch a baby sitting on a pot getting red in the face doing what comes naturally ... the perfect example.

If that's giving voice, what about making speech? Here again we are borrowing from a system which ensures our survival: the digestive system. We use our lips, teeth, tongue, hard and soft palate and the jaw for shaping sound into recognisable words but they are more properly used for biting, chewing and dealing with our daily bread. Yet with those selfsame moving parts we may whisper lovers' secrets, declaim Shakespeare or tell 4B Lower, 'Hurry up, pack up your books and don't bang the chairs'.

You can also think of your voice as an instrument, a wind instrument. This may be a new idea to you, unless you are much given to singing in the bath (a very good exercise, by the way). Let's compare the voice with a double-reed instrument like the oboe. Air is blown through the split cane and as the edges vibrate a note results that moves through the resonating cavity of the oboe. The keys of the instrument, manipulated by the player produce notes of different pitches and what we hear is music. You may well ask why the notes in the hands of a gifted player sound infinitely more wonderful than the notes of certain human voices but look at it this way. It's not just the construction of an instrument but what we do with it and how we take care of it that really matters. Oboes, clarinets, flutes and so on are made mostly of hard materials but if damaged or misshapen will produce a distorted sound no matter how accomplished the musician.

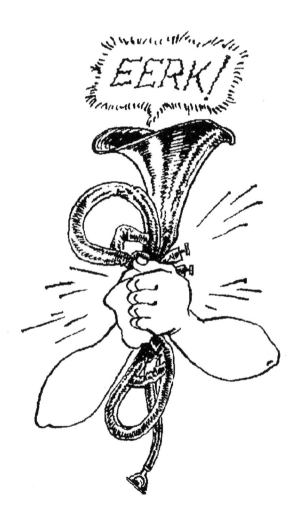

The human voice is air, moulded and resonated by much more flexible stuff so any resultant distortion is often of our own making. The housing is critical, both its condition and shape.

For instance it is common to see speakers thrusting their heads forwards like tortoises peering from their shells, in a mistaken effort to be better heard. To move the sound forward they poke the chin and effectively strangulate the voice. The ways in which we stand, sit and generally hold our upper body are crucial to vocal performance.

Tension is the other enemy. If you are apprehensive your shoulders and neck tighten up, which also affects the jaw, so what chance has your voice of emerging freely? To compound this situation, if the jaw is clamped it becomes difficult to articulate the sound, make the consonants clear so the speech as well as the voice is reduced.

The body and voice work in tandem so it's necessary to begin with considering the body as a whole. So that's where we'll start.

THE REAL WORK

It's odd that we so often think of speaking as a head activity. We think with our brains, and if those thoughts are to be spoken, we open our mouths and out they come. But after the impulse to utter there is a longer journey to be made: the organisation of enough breath, the activating of the cords and the shaping of the sound. How we feel about what we're saying, the situation in which we're saying it and what we expect to happen as a result are all likely to show up in our whole body.

Anyone who uses a lot of physical energy in the course of their work knows the importance of general fitness as well as the practice of particular muscular skills. Teaching may not, at first glance, seem like dancing the lead in *Giselle*, or running a marathon, but it can certainly feel as exhausting. That's why I always like to begin an exercise programme with a consideration of the whole body. By freeing tensions and adjusting posture, energy can flow.

What you are aiming for is your own *natural* voice, unrestricted, flexible and as responsive to your needs as possible. So some of the exercises outlined here are not those which activate muscles so much as unknot them, thus releasing the energy and 'permitting' the voice. There is a real need to eliminate the wrong kind of muscular tension so do not be deceived by the sequence that follows. It may all seem quite easy but it takes care and time to get it right and feel the benefit. At the outset you may also feel quite self-conscious and things may appear worse rather than better. Do not worry. This heightened awareness is only part of the process by which old habits are exchanged for new.

Voice-training is not an exact science. It's more like a journey of discovery; exploring new approaches and sensations, listening to yourself (and others), shifting attitudes and moving the boundaries.

As if this wasn't enough these exercises may have side-effects: they may unclutter the mind and they tend to be good for your heart, your digestion, your nerves and your brain!

If I was only permitted to give six words of advice, they would be these.

STAND UP

BREATHE IN

SPEAK OUT

PREPARATION

1. Have a good stretch, easing out all your tensions. Be aware of your joints and muscles, from your toes right up through your whole body to neck and face.

2. Give your arms a good shake and jump about and jog to some jolly music. Warm up and get the blood coursing.

3. Stand and feel the warmth. Let yourself feel tall with the spine lengthened. Roll the shoulders. Lift and drop them, allowing the arms to be heavy. Have your body weight balanced. Reach the crown of the head up, and let the sides of your body be free and easy. Release any tension in the neck.

Look straight out.

Be uplifted ...

... but hanging.

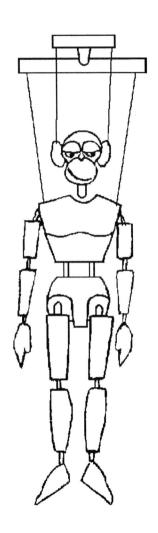

BREATHING

1. In this good stance just become aware of your breathing — quietly. Observe its going out and coming in. Your shoulders should remain relaxed, and, as you breathe in, think of your shoulder blades dropping down, and the front of the chest widening. When breathing deeply don't pull your tummy in. Let it expand too.

2. Let your jaw drop open — just a little. Lick your lips and continue to observe your breathing. The air will feel cool as it goes in and warm as it comes out. Concentrate on the outgoing breath; it is your source of vocal energy.

3. Put one hand on your waist. Involve your vocal cords and let the outgoing breath emerge as a series of sounds like this: *HUH - HUH - HUH* — as many as the breath will allow, and feel them under your hand.

It will sound like a hollow laugh; you can let it be quite strong but don't force it. At the same time, try to imagine a ball bouncing on your diaphragm, or a child using it as a trampoline.

WARMING UP THE SOUND

1. Now that the boiler is going in the basement, so to speak, it's time to turn on the radiators at the other levels. So — with the hand still resting lightly above the waist, on the next breath make the sound a long note: *HU-U-U-U-U-UH*. Feel the vibrations under your hand. Make a few more of these long notes.

Do not push the breath — just *use* it.

2. Place your hand on the upper chest now (the bony bit), and raising the pitch of your note slightly, on the next breath let your jaw drop down, and sound another long note *HA-A-A-A-A-A-AH*, and feel those vibrations under your hand. Do a few of these.

This is the ground floor of your voice.

3. With both hands cupped under your chin and fingers resting gently on the cheeks, take a sizeable breath, raise the pitch slightly and sound *HOO-OO-OO-OO-OO-OO-OOH*. Feel these vibrations in the mouth and through the cheeks.

Imagine yourelf on the first storey.

4. Now, with thumbs resting in ears and fingers on forehead, let the pitch soar up on a long hum *MM-MM-MM-MM-MM-MM-MM*.

Feel the vibrations in your vocal attic.

5. Lastly, play around with the idea of having an elevator in your house, so that you can travel sound smoothly from level to level, moving the heat, the energy, the actual sound, through the resonating spaces of the voice.

MM-MM-MM-MM-MM,

4

HOO-OO-OO-OO-OOH,

3

HA-A-A-A-A-A-AH,

2

HU-U-U-U-U-U-UH,

1

One at a time, or in sequence on sliding scales, but always sensing and experiencing the sound as warm vibrations.

FINDING YOUR NOTE

Every voice has a peculiarly 'right' pitch, a note which is all your own. It is relative to the nature of your cords and the size, shape and condition of your resonating spaces.

It's helpful to be aware of that centre, as your resting place and as your departure point. Don't expect to discover it at once, but bring the idea to mind and explore it.

1. Sit comfortably (but not collapsed), let your spine be lifted and shoulders relaxed. Drop your head forward and feel the tension at the back of your neck this causes. Keeping your chin low, allow your head to roll back into an upright position, concentrating all the time on releasing that tension at the back of the neck. Looking ahead turn the head slowly to right and left; then centre it.

2. Be conscious of your breathing, and as before let the jaw drop a little and concentrate on the outgoing breath.

3. Engage the cords in a gentle and relaxed way. You will probably sound like a dog growling in its sleep.

That's fine; listen to the sound ...

4. Let it grow more purposeful — like dry gargling. Keep listening

5. Let it be a note: *HU-U-U-U-U-U-UH* ... close your mouth on it ... *MM-MM-MM-MM-MM-MM*.

6. Measure your breath into two halves. Sound equally: *HU-U-U-U-U-U-UH — MM-MM-MM-MM*.

This section should all be done quite quietly, in a relaxed way and should be carefully listened to, because here you will eventually find your base note. This will probably be at a pitch just below your most naturally easy speaking voice.

Alternatively, you can try finding your pitch in the place where I have my students search for it — in the waste paper bin.

Pick up a metal bin and empty it. Place it in front of your face and hum quite loudly on a descending scale. You'll probably find a place on the scale where your note becomes very powerful and impressive. That's IT.

If you raise *two* powerful notes one of them is the resonant pitch of the bin. One is yours. You'll almost certainly be able to figure out which is which.

OPENING YOUR MOUTH

1. Give your head a shake — not too violently, just enough to release any tensions.

2. Rub your cheeks — quite vigorously.

3. Drop the jaw. Recall that note in your head. Sigh out and listen hard. Feel the throat open, the way it feels when you're about to yawn.

Carol Mountain — Plea[...]
damaged) with one — [...]

Bi[...]

Caroline [...]

...ughly

[illegible]

Can't get
used to
the singular
form!

compliments

4. Have the jaw easily open (check in a mirror), and sound out on *HA-A-A-A-A-AH*. Keeping the mouth well open (mirror again), raise the centre of the tongue half way through the outgoing *HA-A-A-A-A-AH* and hear it change to *HEE-EE-EE-EE-EEH*.

5. Repeat, visualising the sound waves able to move freely in the wide open spaces of your mouth and throat:

HA-A-A-A-A-AH ... HEE-EE-EE-EE-EEH.

6. Still keeping the mouth well open, bring the lips forward to increase the range of sounds, thus:

HOO-OO-OO-OO-OO-OOH ... AH .. EE.

MAXIMISING THE MEANS OF SPEECH

The **TONGUE** is all muscle and therefore very flexible.

Use a mirror to check what your tongue is doing.

1. Put the tongue out and observe it.

2. Point it, and relax and round it alternately.

3. Using just the tip inscribe a circle with it, barely touching the lips and retaining the open position of the mouth.

4. Shoot it in and out rapidly.

5. Add your voice. *LA-LA-LA-LA-LA-LA*.

The **NOSE** is cartilaginous and the middle of the bony structure of your face.

Think of it as the centre and the means of carrying sound forward.

1. Using a fairly high note, hum forward, pulsing the sound and reaching out with it.

Now... as many of these as the breath will allow

2. *ING-ING-ING-ING-ING-ING-ING*

... a clock striking.

3. *ONG-ONG-ONG-ONG-0NG-ONG-ONG*

... you're a gong.

4. *ANG-ANG-ANG-ANG-ANG-ANG-ANG*

... an American trolley-car.

The **LIPS** are soft and malleable tissue and they are responsible for a great deal of the definition of your speech.

They are also the most visible moving part when we speak.

1. Blow vigorously through them.

2. Now shape them into a 'p' sound and practise it in triplets:
ppp — ppp — ppp — ppp —ppp — ppp.

3. That was just air. Add sound to it and it becomes:
bbb — bbb — bbb — bbb — bbb — bbb.

4. Accent them so:
Bbb — Bbb — Bbb — Bbb — Bbb — Bbb.
bBb — bBb — bBb — bBb — bBb — bBb.
bbB — bbB — bbB — bbB — bbB — bbB.

5. To make the brain work as well, try accenting thus:
     Bbb — bBb — bbB.   Bbb — bBb — bbB.

For further articulation exercise use this same format, and alternate series of voiceless sound (like **p**) with voiced sound (like **b**): **t** and **d** will use the front of the tongue; **k** and **g** will exercise the middle of the tongue (but don't do it with your mouth nearly closed). You can also do triplets of **l** sounds for good measure.

Here are two nonsense words to repeat for practice:

NIMINY (as in 'Jiminy Cricket')

and **TOPOKOTA**
(as in 'To pocket a billiard ball').

Start saying them slowly, then speed up, but keep it neat.

These exercises, if practised assiduously, will establish better habits of stance and breathing, and will provide you with a more assured basis for your sounding and speaking. If the concentration on a particular one is making you tense up, go back to the beginning and repeat the preparation exercises. The chances are that any exercise you find especially difficult will be precisely the one you most need to practise again, or more often.

When the voice is fully exercised and explored then it becomes possible to call on any part of the vocal resource to help make your meaning clearer, adding 'realised' sound to match the words. Words themselves may be anticipated by the listener, or may be quite unpredictable, but a well-tuned instrument colours their intended purpose.

How many ways can a teacher say, 'Good morning', and what do they all mean?

... A further word about BREATHING.

You frequently hear the advice: 'Take a deep breath before you speak'. This has a twofold purpose: to ensure enough air for what you want to say, and to calm you down. So is it always the right advice? Generally yes, though it's a mistake to think you need enormous amounts of air for speaking (singing is infinitely more demanding on the breath). If breathing is open and easy your brilliant brain can judge how much air you need automatically. The *important* thing to remember is that effective vocal sound needs breath behind and under it. Then the voice is properly supported. It's no good letting all the air rush out and then uttering on the last gasp. Nor do you want to gust all over the words so that by using too much, paradoxically, you sound breathless.

So, breathing exercises (which will increase your capacity anyway) are aimed at ease of flow and comfortable control. Good posture, absence of tension, and awareness of an open throat are all part of sensible practice. Ultimately you build a proper support system which makes all speaking easier. You then arrive at maximum effect for minimum effort (one of my guiding principles in life).

As for the nerve-calming, that's true too, but there are some exceptions. I used to teach at an all-male college and have known P.E. students, anxious to display the amazing capacity of their manly chests, show off at the breathing exercises, hyper-ventilate and keel over like daffodils in the wind.

Children hyper-ventilating need to re-balance their gases, so should be asked to breathe in and out of a paper bag. Again, if someone is having an asthma attack it does *not* help them to be told 'Keep calm and breathe deeply'. In this instance it's usually better if they take small high breaths into the nose and mouth, rather than labour the lower respiratory tract.

But remember the message is still

STAND UP

BREATHE IN

SPEAK OUT

SPACE TRAVEL

Teachers talk and talk ... and TALK. That's what the job demands. As well as powers of endurance teachers also need many different voices. You have to be leader, judge, comforter, entertainer and occasional star. You have to order, persuade, explain (for the umpteenth time), scold, encourage and inspire. Your voice has to do all this *and* at the right moments.

Meeting the needs of children and students in your care makes every day potentially exhilarating and potentially exhausting. You really *do* need the strength of an ox, the hide of a rhinoceros and the patience of a saint. So why should you choose to become a teacher? That's a question I'm not going to answer. And how can you make sure your voice is up to it? That one I'll try.

I absolutely believe that you need to know something of the workings of the voice, to think of it as part of your total physicality and understand what kind of exercises will release your vocal power. The knowledge is useful; the practice is essential. For some it will happen easily; for others it will be more hard won.

But in the last analysis it's up to you. Only *you* can learn by asking, listening, reading. Only *you* can explore the possibilities by exercising and experimenting. Only *you* will then experience the changes and the freedom. If that sounds too great an ambition it's because I also believe in aiming high!

It's only by recognising and measuring the task that you can tackle it with confidence. As the Bard says ' ... the readiness is all'. Let's move on now and look at an obvious reality of the job.

Teaching frequently means talking in big spaces to large numbers, who are not always in a perfect state of hushed expectancy. These are three factors which often hang together. When this happens to a teacher for the first time instinct and old conditioning sometimes take over. You want to be heard of course. Remember when you were a child and your Granny, who didn't hear so well, came to tea? When you had a line to speak in your first school play? When, as a senior, you had to give a vote of thanks to the visiting speaker? That insistent little voice from your mother, your teacher comes back to you as you face a hall full of restless students. 'Speak up,' it tells you,'SPEAK UP, SPEAK UP.' So you clear your throat (your first mistake, but we'll return to that later) and you endeavour to speak UP. You do this by jutting out your chin (second mistake) and raising the pitch of your voice. The result doesn't sound like you at all, which is alarming, so you try harder, get more tense and up goes the pitch again. We are not talking about up an octave, or off the scale or anything like that but enough to mean you are making it more difficult for yourself and that your voice will tire more quickly. Of course you'll learn from this experience ... or will you? So much of what we do vocally is habitual that you might continue to approach this situation in the same way and perpetuate the problem.

Start again ... If you've got a 'frog in your throat' don't try and get rid of it by rasping away at your poor cords; swallow it instead. That's much more soothing. Then listen to this injunction. SPEAK OUT. OUT ... not UP. But first take a good breath in and feel it swelling your lower chest, not lifting your shoulders but swelling your chest, and imagine the ghost of a smile beginning on your lips (which you may also lick to release the tongue). Let the breath out while you look around the hall in as calm a manner as you can. Make it clear you are ready, but waiting until *they* are. Take another good breath, look firmly towards the middle of the assembly and speak, thinking of your voice travelling all the way to the back. Don't rush off at speed. It's not an exact equation but the advice guideline is 'the bigger the space ... the slower you speak', especially at the start. It's a two way 'tuning-in' process: you tuning into the space and them tuning in to you.

It's also true that in a large space it's harder for those at the back to see you clearly so it's wise to keep relatively still. This does not mean rooted to the spot but it does mean not wagging your head irritatingly, or fidgeting or pacing up and down like a caged tiger. People need to be able to focus on you. Naturally you will now cite examples of speakers who are highly successful in spite of going off like a rocket and whirling like a dervish. This advice is for ordinary mortals and not for rule breakers.

Those of you who have been lecturing or teaching for a long time will have resolved the problems, mastered the space and the crowd. That's fine but check the points anyway just in case something applies.

PUTTING IT ACROSS

'Projection' is that elusive quality of speaking in a way which makes other people listen to you. There is more than one factor involved. You have to pay attention to the physical business, and you have to be committed to your material.

Both what you say and the way you say it add up to the successful delivery of your message.

Let's first consider the practical elements; those which ensure that you will be heard.

BREATH.

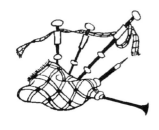

You need enough of it, and you need it under control. To be very loud you obviously want plenty of breath, but it's the properly controlled passage of air through the cords that matters. If you release too much as you speak you will merely sound 'out of breath'. If you hold it in too much you will sound strained.

'Enough puff '— but not too much.

CORDS.

Posture and alignment of the neck is crucial so that the throat is open. Using your natural middle pitch, (that's the one that sounds and feels strong and comfortable) will then ensure that you don't force the voice or harm the cords.

Shape up — 'go with the flow'.

RESONANCE.

It needs to be well balanced, neither booming in the chest nor whining through the nose. To make sound travel feel the vibrations reverberating through the bony mask of the face.

It's called 'using your head'.

ARTICULATION.

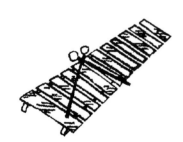

No amount of well-controlled breath and properly balanced resonance will be enough if the pronunciation of the words is fudged. Don't be afraid to open your mouth, and do put in all the consonants; they will carry the day. This is not mouthing, elocuting or anything affected like that.

Think of it as using '**a bolder type face**'.

Is being heard *enough?* ... Well no, it's not. Hearing the words is one thing; comprehending their intention is another. You know how you can be listening to someone giving a speech (a practised speaker who knows what he or she is doing), but you find that your mind has wandered off. You're not with the argument or, for that matter, with the speaker. Though the words are clear enough something is missing.

What?

That's what we need to identify.

It is the mental effort of involving the listener, the emotional impulse which connects argument with audience. It's the *will* of the speaker, not only to be heard, but also to be understood. That *will* has to be there before you open your mouth, and still there after the last word has died away. Obviously it's easier to apply this to an impassioned plea for a cause close to your heart, than to give instructions on how to follow the fire-drill. Nonetheless that 'total packaging' is part of projection, a critical part.

It's a quality of 'wholeness' ... the ring of conviction.

There are differences between the one-off occasion (a special lecture, or talk perhaps) and the on-going everyday nature of teaching. There are *huge* differences in the desire and ability of individuals to hear and absorb what you're saying.

Teachers want to optimise their chances, make real contact, go home satisfied ... *and* with the voice intact.

TO WHOM IT MAY CONCERN

All lecturers and teachers have the voice as their first and most vital resource. All expect and hope to be listened to. All have numbers of students or children in their care, and will develop personal styles and strategies as they pursue their careers. Most will find themselves constantly having to re-evaluate the job and themselves as they go along. But there are differences: of demand, of the nature of the work, of particular skills appropriate to the age levels. You would be as unlikely to lecture an infant as you would be to teach nursery-rhymes to a post-graduate student. Content aside, formal and informal methods require appropriate modes of speaking for different groups. Size, both of teachers and children, is a factor. For instance it's not unusual for a pint-sized secondary teacher to feel that the torso of a burly fifth-former is not a suitable part of the anatomy to address. Similarly a teacher of six-foot-three might need to fold into a hairpin bend in order to come face to face with a five year old.

It's just a matter of 'sizing up the situation'.

TO THE LECTURER

The route to a lectureship is likely to have been an academic path. Travelling it you will have spent long hours researching, and writing-up in quiet libraries. Although you may have been a brilliant scholar, have studied hard and richly deserve the status you have acquired, it could still come as some-

thing of a shock to find yourself face to face with your first lecture hall full of students. It's your turn now to stand and deliver ... a moment of truth.

Now you must share your scholarship, your theories, your knowledge. This is performance-time, and no self-respecting actor would step out on stage to play 3rd Knight-on-the-left, let alone King Lear, without first preparing both body and voice. Teachers have had at least some monitored Teaching Practice before taking up a post in school. Are you prepared? Have you given as much care to the doing of it as to the thinking about it?

This may need recognition, help and application. It's by no means the case that the cleverest people make the most interesting speakers though they should have interesting things to say. They may be quite at ease in a tutorial situation, and they may be at their best on the written page, but when it comes to the platform they may need to start again in the First Grade for vocal and presentation skills.

TO THE SECONDARY TEACHER

Before you reach the 'chalkface' you will already have used you voice in a variety of ways. It started the moment you stepped inside the school gates. On your way to the Staffroom you may have quelled a riot in the playground, called for hush in a corridor, paused to sort out (more quietly) a student's personal problem ... and you haven't even taken your coat off yet! After the bell there'll be registers to take, students to settle down, work to explain and so on and so on and so on. Your voice should be adjusting all the time   to fit the occasion. Your students, and that will include the bully, the slow learner and the high flier, present you with their varying needs and you are the authoritative voice, whether you are speaking to them singly or collectively. That authority demands sensitivity and confidence. Those attributes are made manifest largely through the voice.

A good and experienced teacher will not need to strain the voice, and quiet firm speaking is more likely to produce a well-ordered class. The sound of confidence is catching and we feel safe in the hands of someone who sounds as though they know what they're doing.

Conversely, an anxious new teacher will often try too hard; notes of panic may be heard and that may well trigger an unfavourable response from the class.

Take starting off ... you walk into a classroom full of noisy, boisterous students, bumping into tables and each other, dropping books and generally looking like a rough sea of disaster. If you're new to the game, a probationer perhaps, you will immediately try to impose your will on this muddle by using your voice.

You launch yourself into a no-win contest.

No single voice (with the possible exception of a Pavarotti) can hope to compete with thirty young healthy ones. If you hurl yourself into this maelstrom and wave your arms at it you'll end up conducting but not controlling. Better stay cool, stand your ground (try not to grit your teeth(and find a non-vocal strategy. That could be rapping the desk, clapping your hands, running up a flag, standing on your head (No, that's probably too much)

... If you have the courage stand absolutely still and silent, and use only your eyes.

You'll find your own best way in the end but what is to be avoided is the shouting match, which simply raises the temperature in the classroom and just makes things worse. If you've forced your voice at the outset it will be hard to 'come down' from there, to relax and find your comfortable level again. A quiet but positive voice is preferable and will be more likely to generate a calm atmosphere. The young copy naturally and need authoritative example. Your manner of speaking may well determine their manner of behaviour.

TO THE PRIMARY TEACHER

You are more in loco parentis than secondary teachers. You will be wiping noses and mopping tears as well as reading books and telling stories. Primary school children do not have exclusive rights to stories of course but it is a more usual part of their education. This requires particular vocal skills and I shall deal with it later.

You will be familiar with the concept of 'busy noise' only you can decide when that becomes uncomfortable noise. There is a point at which it's counter-productive and you may start forcing your voice in order to overcome it. Use your ear to stay within a situation which is tolerable for you.

Children need to recognise the value of quiet (silence too) and appreciate different, and appropriate levels of sound.

Now I'd like to share a worry with you: — 'singing'.

When I am teaching my post-graduate students there is a recurring scenario ...

Me. Now we've finished our warm-up and breathing exercises we're going to sing a round.

Student. Er, I'm sorry ... I can't sing ... I'm tone-deaf.

Me. What does that mean exactly? Are you, in fact, deaf?

Student. Well, no ... but I can't sing ...

Me. Since when?

Student. (confidently) Oh, since primary school.

If you go into the reception class in the Christmas term you will find children enthusiastically singing 'Away in a Manger' in what Laurie Lee famously described as a 'wreckage of keys'. The further up the school you go the more accurately the children are managing to sing the notes. But in the top class, where practically everyone has got it right, there will be a lone voice singing a more original tune. It's nearing the end of the term and the teacher in this class is saying brightly, 'Well done. Now at the concert next Tuesday I want you, Peter dear, (singling out the original tune with an unerring glance) to stand on the end of the back row. You can open and shut your mouth but don't sing. You see, (in a stage whisper) you're tone-deaf and you wouldn't want to spoil it for the others, would you?

Student. (excitedly) Yes, that's it. That's just what happened to me. She said I was tone-deaf ... she said I couldn't sing.

This is where I usually go into orbit and describe, in ways too horrible to repeat here, what I'd like to do to that teacher. For the truth is that though we learn to speak by an imitative and spontaneous process we learn to sing, as we learn to read and write, more formally. It's easier for some than it is for others. Some give up from choice, others have a natural gift. But a few have had the door (between the ear and the brain) slammed shut by a thoughtless primary school teacher.

I have met, over the years, too many people who have been condemned to a lifetime of believing that they couldn't sing. That's sad. One of my mature students was just such a victim, and I challenged him by saying that I could prove to him that he was not tone-deaf. After a few sessions of pitch-training and practice, he arrived one day, grinning from ear to ear. 'Last night,' he said, 'I sang to my children ... and they didn't laugh.'

I treasure that memory.

INDOORS AND OUT

Teachers spend the larger part of their working lives indoors, in halls, in classrooms, laboratories, gymnasia and swimming pools. Each location has its own particular hazards for the voice. Consider for a moment the problem of the music-room. A friend of mine who is an expert in this field described it as 'a place where the children have all the heavy artillery, and the teacher has the comparative pea-shooter' (Tony Wenman). The only solution is for the owner of the pea-shooter to establish, *before* work starts, the visual sign language which can control both children and the progress of the music - as all conductors know, very useful practice for future musicians and choir-members. This is 'organised noise', a phenomenon well-known to music and drama teachers. As you carefully orchestrate a huge crescendo, or skilfully direct an impressive battle scene, you may well discover that your enthusiastic pursuit of this phenomenon is not properly appreciated by your colleagues in adjoining classrooms. So the nature of the work, the space itself, the equipment within that space are all factors to be considered. Working out of doors (the sports field and the playground) presents yet more challenges.

IN THE HALL

The need to focus attention and to pace yourself have been established, but it's worth considering again the physical requirements of dealing with the acoustic. The skills of projecting the voice successfully are manifold. (I do not apologise for repeating myself here. If a thing's worth doing, it's worth mentioning more than once.)

First, you must have sufficient breath. It must also be controlled so that the effect is neither of the air spilling out over the words (breathy delivery), nor so held in as to be heard as strangulated.

Secondly, the voice needs to be well resonated in order that it will have carrying power and enrichment. A little extra nasal resonance helps.

Thirdly, the consonants must be well articulated. This does not mean over-mouthing, but placing a positive charge into the words.

Lastly, it's an act of will: the will to be listened to, the will to be heard.

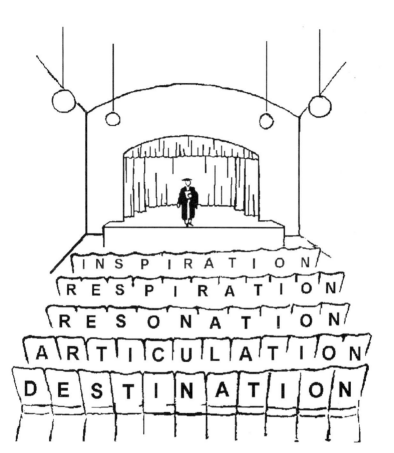

INSPIRATION
RESPIRATION
RESONATION
ARTICULATION
DESTINATION

IN THE CLASSROOM

Classrooms will vary in size and the quality of their acoustics, and you have to be sensitive to those differences. It's largely a matter of luck rather than design. The disposition of the furniture and the students however may well be more under your control. Whenever possible organise the space to be as comfortable to speak in as you can.

In 'the good old days' when boards were supported on easels, it was easy to manoeuvre them to your advantage, but once someone hit on the idea of fixing them to the wall that advantage was lost. Now you are condemned to placing yourself in that most vulnerable of positions: 'Sir or Miss with Back to Class'. Behind you a range of opportunities exists; notes can be passed, missiles exchanges and war can break out. Every teacher must sort out a strategy for using the board. Either prepare it beforehand, or ensure that time taken up by writing is brief and well divided, or make someone else do it - but this you *must* remember: if the face is out of sight the voice may be out of mind. It's perfectly fine to repeat what you are writing (though it's wise to adjust the volume acordingly and sharpen up the articulation), but leave the important message to be delivered face to face.

I must not turn my back on the class
I must not turn my back on the class
I ot turn my back on the class
turn my back on the class

When using other visual aids, OHPs, flip-charts, videos etc. you will frequently be speaking as well. The advantage of these is that you can remain looking forwards, though the focus will be off your face and on the presented image, which of course is where you want it. The trick here is choosing the right words and emphasis to make it clearer and knowing when to let the picture or diagram speak for itself.

A general rule is put your maps, diagrams and tangible objects where everyone can see them, don't hide behind them and don't talk to *them* rather than the class.

There are other dangers with audio-visual equipment: collapsing charts, electrical faults, jamming slides which is why I tend to avoid them and rely on the human voice.

THE SCIENCE LABORATORY

Ever since my eldest son nearly lost an eye in a school laboratory accident, I have felt very strongly about the absolute imperative of ensuring that instructions are clearly and accurately given. A misunderstood or half-heard message simply will not do. There is combustible stuff around in a lab. My office at home constantly reminds me of that, as the view from my window across a school playground looks straight into a science block, where flames from the Bunsens can clearly be seen.

Naturally the equipment in a lab (benches, burners etc.) tends to be fixed so children working at them will frequently have their backs turned away from the teacher. Furthermore, they will often be concentrating hard on the job in hand so will be less 'tuned' to listen. Then again, the names of some chemicals closely resemble the names of others, and that should give us pause for thought. So my advice to all teachers of science is this: you must move the students where they can all see you, both to hear what you say, and to follow any demonstration you may be making before letting them loose on the equipment. This may only mean turning them round, but make it your business to speak very clearly, especially when pronouncing the names of the apparatus or the materials involved in experiments.

Similar problems may be encountered in the teaching of Art, I.T., Wood and Metalwork, particularly the last two where potentially lethal machinery is involved and where you face the additional problem of noise. It's not easy for a voice to compete with a bandsaw or power drill. The solution to the problem is a proper awareness of the children's point of view, their inadequacy and vulnerability. Maximise your chances by moving whatever you appropriately can, and take time and trouble to make all instructions absolutely clear.

It's all commonsense really but, like a good deal of that, it is also worth repeating.

THE GYM

The gym is predominantly the province of the Sports Department, but may be used by other teachers for Drama, Singing and other events.

The larger space does not mean so much increased volume so much as clearer articulation, more head resonance (not higher pitch), and speaking more slowly. This last is particularly true in spaces which echo. When there are plenty of people to absorb the sound that problem is lessened so it's easier to address a full hall that a small group at the far end of the gym.

It can be encouraging to test your voice in an empty hall. You'll need an ally. Start by standing three feet away from your listener and speak in your normal voice. Turn and walk ten paces away, then turn around and talk exactly as before. Keep repeating the process, letting the voice feel free and forward. Put energy into the words but don't speak more loudly or raise the pitch. You may be agreeably surprised to see how far away you can be before you need to do anything drastic.

SWIMMING POOL

These are notoriously the worst places to speak in. Water reflects sound as well as light and there are hard shiny surfaces eveywhere creating a real echo chamber - to say nothing of all that splashing and shrieking!

It's best to establish clear signalling systems beforehand, so that students can respond to whistle blasts or gestures, which will tell them to be on the left, on the right, in the water or out of it.

Some teachers use loud hailers which help to direct the voice, but here body language is really the order of the day.

THE FIELD

On the pitch arm signals are a time-honoured part of the game, so cricket umpires and linesmen can relay messages without ever opening their mouths. Coaching though is different because it's likely that you'll be running up and down as well. That will make you conscious of your breathing, so when you need to comment remember it's that outgoing breath you are using. Try to sense it bouncing off your diaphragm, coming from the centre of the body, and cultivate a feeling that the sound is resonating straight through the bones of the face. It sometimes helps to visualise sound so imagine your words flying like an arrow to a specific target.

Out of doors you are going to have to use more volume, because the voice can be grabbed and scattered by the wind. If you have a lot of speaking to do, gather your flock around you and talk to them at close quarters. Don't forget either that it's better to talk *to* the flock rather than 'address the ball'!

It's the golden rule again — make it as easy on yourself and your voice as possible.

COLOURING IT IN

We've thought about the workings and the moving parts. We've considered some of the challenges to the teaching voice in a variety of situations. We've also looked at some of the common problems and how to overcome them.

Knowing more, being encouraged to take control of your own vocal resource, and exploring new approaches are all excellent ways of gaining confidence; and confident is precisely how you need to sound. Ease of voicing and the sound of positive energy add up to confident performance. You perform when you teach and you often find yourself in the same relationship as a performer with an audience. But there's a critical difference: *your* audience hasn't paid to come in and they don't always want to be there at all.

So ... that's another challenge.

DYNAMICS

I include this section because, apart from skill at playing the notes, an instrumentalist (and you *are* one) needs to make real sense of the music ... the dynamics.

In my dictionary the word 'dynamic' is defined as *'having energy of character'*. I would like to add 'living' to character. In terms of speaking I see it as how we invest words and phrases with sound to give them meaning, weight and stature. The choice of words themselves and the sound with which we colour them is how we give full expression to our intent. As in music, dynamics will incorporate aspects of sound such as speed, volume, pitch and emphasis.

Let us consider a simple question: 'Will you go for a walk?'

EMPHASIS

What happens if we change
the stress?
'*Will* you go for a walk?' Do
you detect a note of
exasperation?
'Will *you* go for a walk?'
Not somebody else but you

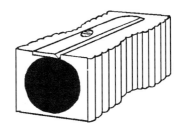

alone.'Will you *go* for a walk?' Not something you would
normally be expected to do.'Will you go for a *walk*?' Not a
jog, a swim, a dance, but a walk.

Emphasis is easy enough to mark and observe but colouring
the speech is a much more subtle process than just leaning on
a particular word.

TONE OF VOICE

Taking that last example
again, what about the
tone you use to express
your intent?

89

Suppose the question is put across in a weary and apathetic way? This might imply that the speaker is extremely bored with the listener. Therefore it will be heard as, 'I'd much rather settle down with a good book, but since you are a guest in my house I'd better suggest we do something to while away the time until you depart.'

If, on the other hand, the vocal tone is imbued with a sense of urgency and excitement, perhaps expressed in a low rapid voice, that says, 'I must get you away from here at all costs, and *soon,* in order to tell you something of great importance and secrecy.'

Or again, the speaker might use a voice of such honeyed and irresistible quality that it can only mean, 'I'd like best of all to remove you from here to another place where we can be alone, and where walking is not what I have in mind at all.'

All that then — and *more* probably — is possible with merely half a dozen simple everyday words. It's salutory here to remind ourselves that for the profoundly deaf who rely on lip-reading the only possibilities for interpretation are the facial clues and body-language that accompany the basic reading of the six words. So much do we depend on 'the dynamics' for our understanding of the spoken word.

THE UNSPOKEN WORD

Consider this scenario. You pass friends in the street and they shout out 'O.K.?' or 'How are you?' and as you speed on (you're in a hurry) you cry 'Fine thanks - and you?' (not waiting to hear the answer). If you had stopped and thought about it the answer might have been very different: 'Well last week I had a nasty cold, which has left me with a dreadful cough which kept me awake half the night. Consequently I'm feeling very tired ... and yesterday I tripped over the doorstep and stubbed the big toe on my right foot; that's still painful and causing me to limp ... and the preoccupied look I'm wearing is because I'm going to see my boss this morning about a rise since I'm having problems keeping up with the mortgage ...'

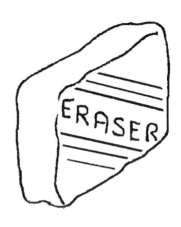

But no!

You say, 'Fine thanks ...' because you recognise that neither you nor your friends have time for a chat and you don't especially want to know how they are *either*.

If we're honest we can admit that a number of our responses are less than fully conscious, automatic even, and that is perfectly acceptable 'social language' — economic and bland.

But we have the whole rich resource of the English language at our disposal for the expression of our thoughts, our dreams and our intentions. There's wealth indeed. In any case teachers have a vested interest in furthering the development of articulacy in those they teach.We sometimes need to think about whether we are settling for a limited vocabulary, and whether we are doing ourselves justice with our personal style of speaking.

THE CONSIDERED WORD

The vocal dynamic will inevitably lead us to a consideration of words.

Suppose you are asked to give a farewell speech for a colleague who is retiring, or an explanation of some fresh research, or deliver the eulogy for a friend, or make an appeal for a worthy cause. You will think carefully about the words you choose. You write them out, change and rephrase them, ask for a second opinion, and lie awake at night worrying whether that really is the best way of expressing your thoughts and feelings.

The English language has many roots and sources and it contains an infinite number of possibilities for being most explicit or most misleading. The way in which we utter it further enhances or depletes those possibilities.

So how can we make our expression more colourful and, paradoxically, our meaning more plain?

The first trick is to listen more intently — to observe with the ears. Try to identify why some speakers compel your attention. The chances are that such speakers give off 'positive energy' through their utterance. Words and phrases will stand out in relief so that the meaning has a kind of third dimension and the message can be easily received. They match perfectly their intention with their delivery. These speakers and their techniques are worth trying to emulate. But that's only half the solution because, of course, *your* voice needs to express *you*, not someone else. It's more a question of 'catching the style' of those positive speakers, and then making it your own.

EXERCISING THE WORDS

That may sound an odd idea, but you *can* exercise words, by experimenting and playing with them.

Make a list of verbs which denote physical action: punch ... kick ... leap ... strike ... Say them quietly, then louder, and then louder still. At the same time do the action. Pause for a moment and think about the words matched with the actions. Now concentrate on the first word ... punch ... Think about what it felt like, what it looked like; and now just speak the word (no action) at a normal pitch and volume. By studying the words separately you should be able to think and hear them more clearly and positively and, with practice, they will gain additional weight, colour and shape.

Obviously not all words lend themselves to this kind of treatment, but verbs of action are often onomatopoeic and are therefore suitable. Take push ... burst ... bang ... for example; they all start with plosive consonants which imply both effort and contained or restrained energy.

This exercise is not intended to lead into 'acting out' all the words you speak; that would be ridiculous and could only end with 'freaking out' rather than 'speaking out'.

It is more like any kind of exercise for a particular part of the body. For instance playing scales will lead to greater strength and flexibility in the fingers, ennabling you to do more with the music. Exercising the muscles of the mouth will improve your speaking and interpretation in the same way.

Now consider some adverbs (those useful words which describe how you do something): lustily ...gently ... sharply ... carelessly ... Speak these at different volumes (as before).

Adverbs usually modify verbs, so attach these; sing ... stroke ... hit ... throw ...

You will probably have been well aware that in changing the volume from very quiet through to very loud, sometimes that was less than appropriate. The verbs will show how that works.

Now we have ... sing lustily ... stroke gently ... hit sharply ... throw carelessly ... Without action try saying these pairs of words at increasing volume and you'll see what I mean. To 'sing lustily' you are bound to be more comfortable at greater volume. Similarly with 'stroke gently' it will feel more appropriate to use less volume.

There is an intrinsic 'rightness' about these examples because of their meaning.

NEXT STEP

Take one verb and that list of adverbs. The verb 'to speak' will provide useful scope. You are now going to practise speaking ... lustily ... gently ...sharply ... carelessly ... Find a piece  of prose, a news item perhaps and experiment speaking it in four different ways. Give the reading the character of each adverb as far as you are able. Does this change the meaning for you? Would it do so for a listener? Do you find yourself automatically speaking higher or lower when you have those adverbs in mind?

These exercises are designed to make you listen more intently, so that you might be able to answer some of those questions. Once you have grasped that you are in charge of imbueing mere words with colour, and whole phrases with mood, you are well on the way to making all your speaking more positive and more interesting.

PITCH AND RHYTHM

I should stress again that changes in normal speech are quite subtle, and it is only in exercise that we may exaggerate to make the point.

Take pitch for instance; unlike singing, which stretches the voice over two octaves or more, in speaking we normally use just a handful of notes, possibly up to five. But within that range an infinite number of gradations and elisions are possible to convey the fullest meaning.

Everyone has a natural pitch to his or her voice which is determined by their physique. But sometimes as a result of habitual tensions the pitch of the voice may be forced either up or down. That frequently causes additional problems which serve to 'lock in' the voice, and deprive it of freedom of expression. With exercise and guidance and a readier ear it is possible to resolve those problems.

That can be a very liberating experience.

For practising purposes, experiment with pitch changes. That will help, not only to increase flexibility, but also to sense where your own natural pitch should be.
Try intoning (that is all the notes on one pitch) a phrase like 'Now I shall sing lustily to you on this note' all the way up a scale — one note at a time.It's very likely that you will find a particular note where your voice feels most confident, and that will mark the middle, or 'natural' pitch.

You may further discover that your natural inclination will be to emphasise the word 'lustily'. There are several factors involved here. The rhythm of the whole phrase has its natural centre on that word; it is the longest word in the phrase; it is of maximum importance to the meaning, and therefore bears the chief burden. All language carries these subtleties of rhythm, and it's good when you identify and sense that, even in such a simple sentence.

When you speak poetry your ability to recognise and respect rhythm becomes critical to your delivery. Speaking verse aloud is good practice, and can afford unexpected pleasure. The language of poetry is often very colourful and concentrated; it is language in distilled form and structured in rhythmic shape. Don't be scared by poetry. You may initially find the classics daunting; you may have been put off at school by having to analyse Shakespeare and Keats. Try some of the modern poets for speaking aloud and you may surprise yourself.

Very often all we need is to put more thinking into our actual speaking, ensuring with the ear that the sound is a true reflection of the mind. The worst delivery is the kind which seems unrelated to anything or anybody, in fact merely mechanical, sounding as though it had neither brain nor heart. You know you could never strike up a relationship with a computerised voice.

Relish the language, explore its riches through increased awareness. Let word, phrase and sound work in perfect harmony.

READING ALOUD

Reading aloud from a text in an interesting and expressive way is not as easy as you might think, nor is it always given enough care and thought.

When you were first learning to read, to de-code print and struggle with long words, you needed to do that out loud. Teachers, and probably parents, helped you to acquire those skills, but as soon as you could read you were allowed to go away and get on with it by yourself. To be literate meant, in effect, to be silent. It also meant you could rattle along as quickly as you could understand the print. Now some people read aloud just like that, and going too fast is one of the commonest problems I encounter. But the activity of reading aloud is not to prove you can do it, but to re-create the words, to make them live off the page. That's quite a different skill and one that a teacher should value properly.

Of course, if you are reading the register or a list of ingredients, you don't need to give a major performance. It is enough to be clear and precise making sure that everyone has heard and understood. Beyond that the human voice can convey confidence in both speaker and material, and that is important in all reading aloud. I have known a number of able and intelligent people who, faced with a text to read aloud, freeze at the very thought. Frequently it transpires that they are the ones who have acquired reading skills a little later than their peer group, suffered agonies of embarassment at having to read in class. Consequently they have never been able to associate the activity with comfortable feelings. Often they will use the book to hide behind and read to the hinge joint or double up and read to the floor.

It is sometimes the case that they have not relished the idea of reading at all, so books offer fewer delights and may only be read as economically as study demands. I would suggest that, apart from the basic need for literacy, it is vital that children recognise the wealth of knowledge, inspiration and fun available to them in books. All of us depended on someone else's ability to read, and if done well it will have been a happy and influential experience. Even when we become literate the reader aloud gives another dimension altogether to the written word. The text gains substance and reality together with an interpretation of the author's intention. So ... whether it be the simplest of childrens' stories or a learned paper on psychology, when you read aloud you are making the written word accessible. Within the idea of access is also the opportunity for enlightenment and erudition, and the firing of the imagination. This is especially true of poetry and drama. Drama is text specifically intended for speech. In an ideal world all children would have their first experience of dramatic text in the theatre, not the classroom. We don't live in such a world but the teacher who can read vividly is more likely to open the door to the world of the classical drama.

What should be your aims?

Your first is to serve the author as well as the listener, to join them together in fact; then to interpret the sense of the text, conveying mood and feeling. You do this, not by 'acting out' the words, but by having absorbed them sufficiently yourself to know which dynamics give the text a chance to live.

Your next is to observe and match the style of the writing. Some authors write in crisp sentences, others in long poetic lines, so you need to find an appropriate mode of speaking which will allow the rhythm of the book to develop.

If you can study and practise beforehand (aloud of course), it will almost certainly go better. Don't hurry ... think of it from the listener's point of view. You are the one with the book and you know what's coming next. Your listeners do not. They need time to take in what you've just said, what you are saying and to anticipate what is to come. Never be afraid to use the 'pause-button' in order to emphasise a point just made, to focus attention or to 'hold the breath' of your story. The tendency to rush lies, I think, in that old feeling that to read is good and to read fast is better.That can only be true of the time when you were acquiring the facility and remains true only when you are reading to yourself.

Always remember you read aloud for the benefit of the listener, not for yourself. That benefit of being read to, or of being told stories, has been diminished in recent times. Early childhood experience used to include books and stories as part of bedtime routine; it was also part of the care of sick and convalescent children. It is hard to measure the sense of comfort and security that such customs give, or the significance in the development of mind and imagination.

The excellent quality of stories performed on television or tape are of value, but simply not the same as the encircling arm of a parent, grandparent, aunt or uncle. The role of the teacher falls somewhere in between modern and old-fashioned practice; their audience may be plentiful but personal involvement with a 'live' reader or storyteller cannot be equalled.

STORY TELLING

Telling a story without benefit of text demands extra skills. So you've nothing to lean on but your wit, your imagination and your powers of engagement.

There have always been stories, and before the advent of the printing press, before illuminated parchments or scrolls, even before all that laborious scratching on the walls of caves, stories were told. They still are, and will continue to be handed on from one generation to the next by amateurs and professionals alike. Welcome the teller of tales! Welcome the storyteller!

But note how both these expressions (the tell-tale and the storyteller) also have derogatory meanings.

Stories may be brief and used to establish or illustrate a point; they may be longer and part of an even greater history, an episode complete but intrinsic to the whole. There are myths and legends which speak to us of other cultures, and our own, which cross the borders between fantasy and truth. There are parables and morality stories which give us an understanding of concepts and ideas. There are personal accounts bringing people and situations alive and into focus. And more ... much more.

Stories often make facts more palatable, and usually easier to remember, so they have enormous educational value. They may also help children deal with the unvoiced anxieties and fears which lurk just out of reach in the corners of the mind. It's possible that these can be externalised and defeated by the spoken word; in stories, ogres can be vanquished, and good can triumph over evil. Stories are not pure escapism but may be a very real way of releasing, exploring and containing ideas. Above all, they may provide a root from which can spring a desire for literacy.

The skill of storytelling shares some of the attributes of reading from a text, the same use of vocal resources for catching attention and 'colouring-in' the material. Incidentally, 'Are you sitting comfortably?' may be an out-dated cliché, but it had a real purpose. With or without a book it's a good plan to settle your listeners and rivet attention before you begin. Watching professional storytellers can show you this wisdom, and more besides. Never be afraid to learn from the experts. That which seems effortless to them is usually earned, and comes from taking it seriously, rehearsing and paying attention to fine detail.

The difference between reading and telling is that you can change and adapt your story when you have no script to follow.

With your eyes 'out front' you can pick up clues, build on response and the whole process becomes organic - at once more open-ended and, paradoxically, more complete. You need a high degree of concentration, a sense of 'being there' and of taking your listeners with you. The more involved you are the more you can convey. It's a medium to explore and to experience and it really does improve and reward you with practice.

Of course personal style develops over the years, but for some basic advice one of the best maxims is this: 'Know your story. Believe in it, and Enjoy it.' This advice I heard many years ago from H. E. Todd, and he was a master of his storytelling craft.

LOOKING AFTER IT

Whether you are starting out in your first teaching job, or poised to become Head of Department or Headteacher, or even if you are beginning to think about what you will do in your retirement, you cannot afford to be without your most valuable asset.

Your voice is precious and you'll always need it, so looking after it makes good sense.

I have outlined some of the conditions which make teaching such a vocally challenging job - the spaces, the numbers, the noise, the variety of roles, and the sheer amount of talking to be done. I have touched on the psychological aspects, the stress and anxiety, the heavy responsibilities and some of the more creative opportunities too. All of these factors lead to some common conditions, but I have not yet mentioned what is possibly the most common. It is the one most frequently complained of by teachers, namely, the 'dry throat'.

Now, it's not to be wondered at that when you are opening and shutting your mouth so much and talking constantly, your salivary glands have a hard time of it keeping your throat properly lubricated; and if you're very anxious or weary they tend to go on strike altogether. It doesn't help either that schools are often overheated and sometimes dusty. You must compensate for some of this. It's quite extraordinary that when people say how dry their throats are that they could probably easily avail themselves of the obvious remedy. They only need to turn on a tap - and water is not expensive.

It may not be practicable to have an immediate supply in every classroom, but there are ways of dealing with that. If I'm lecturing, I usually have my trusty thermos of cold herb tea at the ready. I've been known to sneak it under a lectern ... and even into a pulpit.

Teachers tend to confine their drinking to the staffroom, where they consume quantities of tea and coffee, and sometimes in a smokey atmosphere. None of this is a good idea, since caffeinated drinks are inclined to leach fluid out of the body: coffee is a well-known diuretic.

There is a current theory that many of us in Western society are to some extent permanently dehydrated. That's particularly true of those of us who work in institutions. This is partly due to the central heating of our buildings, and we tend to neglect the regular exercise which works up a good thirst to be quenched. It's healthy to drink plenty anyway to clear the body of toxicity and it will also help deal with that dry throat. So drink more (though not alchohol) and remember that swallowing also opens the throat and relaxes the cords.

In cases of voice-loss, or miserable throat, drink plenty of herb tea ... fennel, mint, lemon-balm, sage, rosemary are all efficacious ... adding a squeeze of lemon and spoonful of honey if you like.

In **THE REAL WORK** section you have a sequence of exercises which will help you take care of your voice and ensure that you don't mis-use or abuse it. Simply because you will use it so much it's a good plan to build some moments of voice awareness and exercise into your daily routine. Eventually this will become such a habit that it will be automatic.

FIRST THING IN THE MORNING

When you wake up have a good stretch and try to include a luxurious yawn to open the throat and the jaw. There's no point in being polite about it, trying to stifle it or cover it with

your hand. Then a good deep breath followed by a big and audible sigh. If your partner asks 'What's the trouble, darling?', you just say (whilst downing a glass of water), 'This is my early morning voice routine.' Hum purposefully while you're bathing, showering, or putting your head under the pump. This will start warming up the larynx.

If you have a long, lazy bath you can indulge in some growls too, or the occasional operatic aria. If your partner asks, 'What's the matter now, darling?' just reply, 'Still part of my voice routine.' They'll soon get used to it. Before you clean your teeth have a quick gargle, and when you drink whatever you drink with your breakfast, don't have it scalding hot, though it will do you no harm to breathe in the steam.

ON YOUR WAY TO WORK

If you walk to work, think about how you do it. Check that your shoulders aren't hunched. Let your arms swing easily, if you're not weighted down with bags ... and if you are, distribute the weight evenly. As you walk, imagine you are moving through the frame of your body, or that you have the horn of a unicorn attached to your upper chest, and let it lead you forward. This will have the effect of gently lifting the upper rib-cage whilst leaving the arms relaxed. Hum quietly as you go, and check that the jaw is not clenched against the prospect of the day ahead.

If you're driving, or on public transport, think about relaxing your shoulders and jaw. Blow quietly to release the lips, and hum, ... if you can do that without alarming your travelling companions.

If you're stuck in a traffic jam, you could massage your cheeks, do some high forward humming, practise NIMINY and TOPOKOTA, ... and try to ignore the chap in the car behind giving you those funny looks.

AFTER SCHOOL

At the end of the school day you may well find your shoulders up by your ears, your teeth clamped shut or grinding, your

back aching with the strain and a frown where your smile should be. Look in the mirror. If you deliberately counteract these conditions in a positive and active way you'll feel much less tired than if you just collapse into the nearest chair taking all the tenseness with you.

At this point you need a place where you can be alone for a few minutes (I usually recommend the lavatory).

Now, stand tall, shake your arms vigorously, roll your shoulders, let your head drop forward, roll it gently from side to side. Put your head back where it belongs, but don't thrust the chin. Lift your arms, stretching them overhead, raise first one, then the other, feeling the lift from the base of the rib-cage. Let the arms come to rest by your sides, bend the knees a little, return to the upright position, ease the shoulder blades back and down, take a deep breath, let the air out with a 'WHOOSH', giving your head a shake, with the face muscles as relaxed as possible. Look in the mirror again and say 'WOW', and then ... smile.

Once you've learnt that sequence of events it will take less time for you to do it than it took me to tell you how!

DURING THE EVENING

If you're sitting over papers, writing up reports, preparing work, marking etc. you know that it's easy to get stuck in the same

position, and it's only when you move that you realise how hard you've been concentrating and how you've seized up. I know because it happens to me.

It's a good idea to make yourself stop at regular intervals, have a stretch, roll the shoulders, make a cup of herb tea, and give your head a little shake. Yes, it does have to do with the voice, because even though you may not be speaking, those habits of small tensions in the neck and jaw will become too fixed and affect your voice adversely the next day.

BEFORE YOU SLEEP

This is the time to relax completely. To release any tensions in the throat and soothe the cords do some downward humming, using about three easy notes (this is an effective remedy for whenever your voice feels strained).

Breathe deeply and slowly a few times, then let your natural rhythm take over. Make sure your teeth aren't clenched and that your jaw isn't locked. Think about all the good bits of the day,

... smile gently

... and sleep.

THE LAST WORD

Almost without exception the voice begins free. Babies yell by opening their mouths wide and just letting the sound out. Burping from their stomachs they can carry on crying for minutes on end, stop quite suddenly, give you a beaming smile and then drop straight off to sleep. They do not appear to suffer from sore throats as a result of this activity. It is an unimpeded use of pure voice.

Getting your head and tongue around the words is a more difficult trick, and learnt a bit later. That can afford some frustration and fury but also huge delight and relish.

Then there comes a time when restrictions begin, and those habits of freedom become overlaid. Your machinery for making noise gets suppressed, structured, formalised.

'Don't talk with your mouth full.'
'Oh, do be quiet.'
'Another word out of you and I'll belt you one.'
'WILL you stop talking.'
'Shut up you children.'
'That's *not* a nice thing to say.'

You remember the process by which we learnt to conform, to fit in, to behave? That type of negation, plus confused messages about response, later emotional turbulence, and sometimes deeply traumatic experiences, can change the way we speak and how we are able to communicate ... can, in fact, close down our voices.

Sometimes we need to look at that again to re-discover what we have lost. The way in which we use our voices and the manner of our speaking is enormously varied. It is dependent on many factors and influences which begin in infancy. To master the art of putting together the many physical processes involved, we use our ears to guide us. That is how we acquired speech, and the ears monitor our own sounds as well as dictating our response to others. Our re-actions are coloured by both the language and the overall impression.

'She sounded absolutely exhausted' (though that wasn't what she said).
'He was really very uptight about something' (but he wasn't giving that away in words).
'The minute she opened her mouth I knew something was going on ... '

All these sub-texts are revealed by the *sound* of the voice.

We arrive in adult-hood sounding and talking the way we do because of our families, our native region, our education, our social circumstances, our perception of ourselves in relation to each other and to our place in the scheme of things.

There are times when you need the 'tricks of the trade' that actors use for overcoming their stage-fright (and don't believe anyone who tells you that real actors don't suffer from stage-fright).

Perhaps you are about to tell off the Fifth-form bully who is inches taller than you, and you want to sound really firm but when you open your mouth a thin wavery sound emerges ...

Perhaps you have inadvertently led a class of primary school children into a difficult and threatening situation, and it is essential that no note of panic should be picked up, even though your heart is pounding and your pulse racing ...

You can learn techniques as actors do and develop your voice more fully. Some of these techniques will over-ride the ills which beset you when complete control of the voice eludes you. You can make life easier for yourself by maximising your chances. You can do that by exercising the moving parts as illustrated in this book.

Reading about it may be a first step. The next might be to seek out a Voice teacher, a class, a workshop or join a dramatic society. Give yourself an opportunity to extend your vocal skills. If you are anxious about the state of your voice see a Speech and Language therapist.

Those physiotherapists who are interested in psychology may tell you that we store exhaustion in our legs and anger in our backs; *I* think we store anxiety and stress in our throats.

I'll tell you a story.

Many years ago I was consulted by a student whose voice seized up whenever she found herself in front of a class. Her voice simply would not do what she wanted at all. In fact she had an extremely pleasant voice, was a very intelligent girl, and well motivated towards a teaching career.

We tried all the usual ploys: breathing techniques, relaxation, compensating articulation, and all these she did well. There was power and flexibility and no apparent problem. But still, on Teaching Practice her jaw would lock, her neck go into spasm and her poor voice become strangulated. It was puzzling to say the least.

We kept talking about the dilemma, and I asked her to think about whether she had experienced anything like it before. She described her childhood, a stable and happy one, and she had not been bullied or had any other problems at school.

Suddenly she remembered something which had happened to her at the age of twelve. She had been involved in a car accident and sustained a whiplash injury; for a full year after she had needed to wear a surgical collar. This memory struck her very forcibly, and we came to the conclusion that what might be happening was that whenever she found herself in a situation where there was any anxiety she automatically took up a defensive position. She would reach metaphorically for that collar, and put it on.

Old traumas can return to haunt but may be put to rest by identification. You may think this all a little far-fetched; I can only record that after we had discussed this fully she never had the problem again.

I have often found it necessary to establish a link between an existing problem and an earlier one.

Sometimes it might be as straightforward as finding that the teacher who speaks through a narrow slit where his mouth ought to be is the one who had a rotten time at the dentist when young. He'd laid down a habit of protecting himself by simply not opening it.

The one who talks in short sudden bursts may be the one born into an extremely voluble family, and low down in the pecking order, who could never get a word in edgeways by any other method. He or she needs to be reminded that they've now left their family and that manner of speaking will not serve them well in a classroom.

Habits have to be reviewed, problems identified and measures taken. For, in the last analysis, children and students deserve to be taught by clear and interesting speakers: by those who say what they mean and sound as though they mean what they say.

So ... STAND UP...

BREATHE IN ...

SPEAK OUT ...

and if you must shout ... shout for JOY!

The Voice Care Network UK offers help and advice to teachers, through practical workshops conducted by its members, who are all experienced Voice Teachers or Speech and Language Therapists.

For more information and a contact number in your area write initially to:

The Co-ordinator
Voice Care Network UK
29 Southbank Road
Kenilworth
Warwickshire
CV8 1LA

CAN YOU HEAR ME AT THE BACK?
By Caroline Cornish

Copies of this book are obtainable by mail order. Simply complete the form and send together with the correct payment to:

BiVocal Press
PO Box 246
Exeter
EX1 2YF

NAME _____

ADDRESS _____

_____

_____ POSTCODE _____

Contact telephone no. _____

Occupation _____

Organisation _____ (if applicable)

	TOTAL
No. of copies required at £7.50 per copy	
Post & packing at £1.25 per copy	
TOTAL	

Cheques/PO's should be made payable to: **BiVocal Press**

Please allow 14 days for delivery.